DATE DUE

ETHEL PHILLIPS LIBRARY
SACRAMENTO CITY UNIFIED SCHOOL DISTRICT
SACRAMENTO, CALIFORNIA

Flying Pieces of Macaroni & Cheese!

By
Jeanne Smither Osio

Illustrated by
Lisa Osio Lavin

KyKat Publishing

FLYING PIECES OF MACARONI & CHEESE!

Copyright © 2010 by KyKat Publishing
www.KyKatPublishing.com

All rights reserved. No part of this book may be used or reproduced in any manner without written permission except in the case of brief quotations used in critical articles and reviews. Printed in South Korea on acid-free paper. For more information, please contact KyKat Publishing at PO Box 312, Pacific Grove, CA 93950.

Library of Congress Catalog Card Number: 2010900372
ISBN: 978-0-9843530-0-2
1st Edition

For Kyle and Katherine

Flying Pieces of Macaroni & Cheese

The dog's gone and done it! I see that he's,
Made a mess from his ears way down to his knees!
Won't somebody try to stop him, please?
He's eaten up all my macaroni and cheese!

I gave that naughty dog a squeeze.
With a great big mouthful, he began to sneeze.
Save yourself, 'cause it's in the breeze,
Flying pieces of macaroni and cheese!

Sail on out to the open seas,
Farther and farther till you feel at ease.
Far enough to hide from these,
Soaring bits of macaroni and cheese!

I've asked everyone from Fred to Louise,
From Rome to New York, clear down to Belize.
It seems everyone I've talked to agrees,
The world is now covered with macaroni and cheese!

The dog simply said, "You must never tease,
Or get upset and start to squeeze.
But being covered with macaroni and cheese,
Is <u>so</u> much better than covered with fleas!"

Lonely Spider

The spider sat in her web, her home,
Wondering why she was always alone.
A fly felt sorry for that lonely spider.
He flew to the web to sit down beside her.
"A friend!" cried the spider, as she ran to greet him.
A few minutes later, she decided to eat him.
The spider sat in her web, her home,
Wondering why she was always alone.

The Twister of Fear

The scariest ride at the fair this year,
Was the fastest ride, The Twister of Fear.

Reaching speeds that were death defying,
Absolutely, positively terrifying.

I yelled, I trembled, I shuddered, I cried,
I screamed, I shook, I was petrified!

My face was drenched from sweat and tears,
My pulse was pounding inside my ears.

I covered my eyes, I cringed, I shivered,
I held my breath, I gasped, I quivered.

I almost threw up and that's the truth,
But, bravely, I stepped up to the ticket booth.

Merry McQuid

She painted sunsets and oceans and trees,
Artist Merry McQuid.
Her friends cried, "Merry, paint me! Paint me!"
So Merry McQuid, did.

Bottomless-Pit Pete

"All You Can Eat Just $4.92!"
They didn't know who they were offering that to.

Bottomless-Pit Pete walked in through the door,
And sat down to eat at a quarter to four.

Nine hours later at a quarter to one,
Pete wasn't through, nowhere near being done.

The food was all gone, but Bottemless-Pit Pete,
Remembered the sign read, *"All You Can Eat!"*

Pete was still hungry, and feeling perplexed,
So he first ate the tables, and then the chairs next.

The owner cried, "Leave! You've eaten it all!"
But Pete didn't stop till he ate the last wall.

Hot Dog!

Have you ever heard a hot dog sneeze?
Mine did last night when I added some cheese.
I was quite astonished, but let me embellish,
I heard it burp when I added the relish.
And then this little hot dog fellow,
Looked up at me and said, "Hello."
As I sliced up the onions to finish the job,
My amazing hot dog started to sob.
My fantastic new friend looked ever so sad,
But I have to admit, it didn't taste bad.

Identity Crisis

I gave my dog some cat food,
He meowed and climbed a tree.
I gave my cat the canary's food,
She sang and flew to me.

I gave the canary the rabbit's food,
She hopped right out of sight.
I gave the rabbit some hamster food,
He ran in a wheel all night.

My brother saw the animals,
And said he was going to tell.
I made him a sandwich of turtle food,
And now he just hides in his shell.

Help!

Can someone find my homework?
I know I put it here.
I think the dog must have eaten it,
It couldn't just disappear.

Can someone find my jacket?
I thought it was on my bed.
But there's a pile of other clothes,
That are lying there instead.

Can someone find my rainboots?
I know it rained last night.
I looked beneath a pile of books,
Beachball, puzzles and kite.

Can someone find my lunchbox?
Where did I see it last?
I thought it was in my closet,
I really must find it fast!

Can someone find my backpack?
Last night it was on my floor.
I've looked underneath all my toys,
Socks and shoes galore.

Can someone PLEASE find ME?
I suddenly start to shout.
I came in my room to search for my things,
And can't seem to find my way out!

Motorcycle Minnie

Motorcycle Minnie rides ever so fast,
The wind whipping through her hair.
Flying along at breakneck speeds,
And grinning from here to there.

Over the highways and over the byways,
She speeds along mile after mile,
On country roads and mountain passes,
And always with a smile.

Riding her bike, Minnie's free as a bird,
As the road flies by beneath.
Smiling and grinning, you'll know it's Minnie,
By the bugs between her teeth.

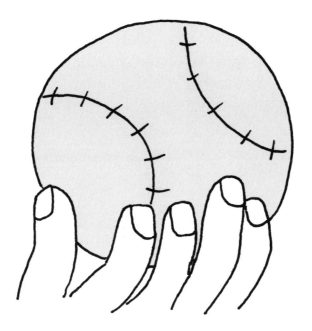

Helping Hand

The thumb and the fingers tried throwing the ball,
But it didn't go quite as planned.
So, the thumb and the fingers cried out for help,
"Will someone please give us a hand?!"

The "Gotcha"

When the moon is high and the stars shine bright,
I tiptoe through the house in the middle of the night.
I know what I want. I know what I crave.
High on the shelf, I have to be brave.

I pile up the chairs... one, two and three,
And carefully climb to the top till I see,
That wonderful, beautiful, delightful jar,
That holds the cookies out of reach up so far.

Excited, I think about what I might find.
Yummy images dance through my mind.
Chocolate chip, peanut butter, I'll have just a few...
Snickerdoodles, butterscotch, cocoa-kisses, too.

But danger lurks at the bottom of the jar,
Under ginger snaps and a sweet lemon bar.
If I reach on in, without asking first,
The end could be bad, maybe the worst!

I know what's down there, 'cause my friend told me.
It happened to her brother's friend's cousin, you see.
While sneaking a cookie from <u>her</u> Mom's cookie tin,
Something grabbed her and pulled her on in!

As the story goes, that was the end.
It seems she was never heard from again.
They say that the cookie jar "Gotcha" will getcha!
If you're not careful, it just might catch ya!

But the thought of those cookies, so gooey and sweet,
My hand creeps closer to the irresistible treat.
I remove the lid, slip my hand in the jar,
My fingers wrap around the sweet lemon bar.

But something has grabbed me, starts pulling me in!
My arms disappear and there goes my chin.
My shoulders are next, will it stop at my knees?
I yell very loudly, "Someone help me, please!"

But my head's in the jar, so no one can hear.
This might be the end, I suddenly fear.
My middle's devoured, and now my legs, too.
But it stops at my feet, 'cause they will not fit through!

The "Gotcha" can't get me, as hard as it tries,
My feet are too big, much to my surprise!
It lets go of my legs, my middle, and then,
I'm finally back out of the jar once again.

My advice to you and to **your** appetite,
Don't try to sneak cookies in the middle of the night.
You'd better think twice when you crave something sweet,
The "Gotcha" will getcha, if you don't have big feet.

Nuts

The peanut played tennis,
The walnut played baseball,
The almond played golf,
The cashew played football.
The pecan played nothing,
'Cause **he** was a clutz,
But he longed to be,
Like the other sports nuts.

Fudge

I wished on a wishbone and make no mistake,
I blew all the candles out on my cake.
I gave my four-leaf clover a nudge,
And wished that whatever I touched turned to fudge.
I touched my skates and I touched my bike,
I touched my little brother, Mike.
I decided to rest on my sweet little bed....
But, my biggest mistake was scratching my head!!

Remember to Forget

How can I ever forget,
My scary dream last night?
I think I dreamed in color,
Or was it black and white?

Ten monsters tried to catch me,
Or were there only three?
They chased me down a beach,
Or was it up a tree?

The monsters had three eyes,
Or was it only one?
I was extremely scared,
Or was I having fun?

I'm feeling so confused,
I'm starting to get upset.
It seems I can't remember,
What I'm trying to forget!

Bricks

The best brick layer in all the world,
Never received a prize.
And no one ever hired him,
Which, of course, is no surprise.

It seems when he built his very first house,
He did all the work from within,
And after he layed the very last brick,
He was never ever seen again.

Arf Mail

I saw a dog with a box on his head,
Into the post office he walked.
Amazed at him,
I followed him in,
And couldn't believe when he talked!

The postmaster acted like nothing was strange.
The dog asked very nicely,
"How much does it weigh?
How much should I pay?
I need to know very precisely."

The postmaster took the large brown box,
And placed it on the scale.
"Two dog biscuits from you,
Will certainly do."
And the dog left wagging his tail.

Ring-a-Ding

Ring-a-Ding had rings on her fingers,
And rings on all her toes.
She had many rings through both earlobes,
And a couple through her nose.

Her bellybutton had three large rings,
There were two attached to her lip.
She had two rings on each eyebrow,
And three more on her hip.

You'd think this is how she got her name,
Because of all the rings.
But, as it turns out, with the slightest move,
Ring-a-Ding, ring-a-ding-ding-dings.

My Stuff

My lost cell phone wasn't under my bed,
But I saw many things that were there instead.
The broken arm from my rocking chair,
An old hair brush with a wad of my hair.
Toenail clippings and a watermelon rind,
Half of a sandwich, don't ask me what kind.
My lost gym sock with the hole in the toe,
The one I lost three months ago.
Dog biscuit, pencil, an old tennis shoe,
A piece of pizza that was now green and blue.
A towel, a slipper, an old soda can,
A cereal bowl and a frying pan.
My snake wrapped around the leg of the bed,
With a bag of corn chips under his head.
A peanut butter jar, a banana peel,
My mother's old shoe that is missing the heel.
My homework assignment I never turned in,
A button, a fly swatter, a safety pin.
A quarter, two pennies, a dust-covered nickel,
A book, a flashlight, a fuzz-covered pickle.
My phone wasn't there, but I was happy to see,
Everything else looked in order to me.

Summer Vacation

School is out
For summer vacation!
It's time for fun
And relaxation.

There's a zillion things
To do for fun.
And lots of time
To get them done.

I'll go to the beach
And to the zoo.
I'll camp outside
And skateboard, too.

I'll build a fort
Up in the trees.
But first I think,
I'll get some zzzz's.

Through the sprinkler,
I'll run so fast.
A 4-leaf clover,
I'll find in the grass.

I'll run barefoot
Without my shoes.
But first I think,
I'll take a snooze.

I'll go for a swim
Down at the lake.
I'll teach my dog
To roll over and shake.

I'll run a race
To see who's best.
But first I think,
I'll get some rest.

I'll take a jog
Around the block.
I'll rollerblade,
I'll take a walk.

I'll stare at my friend
Till someone blinks.
But first I think
I'll catch some winks.

Up a mountain,
I'll take a hike.
Plant a garden,
And ride my bike.

I'll make a kite,
See how it flies.
But first I think,
I'll close my eyes.

I'll go to the park,
Climb on the bars.
I'll stay up late
And count the stars.

I'll turn a cartwheel
Out on the lawn.
But first I think,
I need to yawn....

There's lots of time
To get things done.
Lots of time
To have some fun.

But first I need
To get some sleep.
Don't wake me up.
Don't make a peep.

Now I'm awake,
But something's wrong.
Don't tell me I slept
ALL SUMMER LONG!?

Violent Chef

The kitchen is a violent place,
The chefs are rather mean.
They beat the eggs at a furious pace,
Chop the nuts and whip the cream.
Squeeze the oranges, mash potatoes,
Shread the lettuce and pound the steak.
Press the garlic, slice tomatoes,
Carve the turkey and shake the shake.
Grind the pepper, grate the cheese,
Dice the onions and boil the rice.
Smother the roast in carrots and peas,
Stuff the pork chops and crush the ice.

As you can see, they're not very nice.

Rollercoaster?

Loop – d – loop,
Hold on tight,
Flip on over,
Pull to the right,
Flip again,
Slide on through,
Rollercoaster ride?
No, I'm tying my shoe!

Glup

At 6 years old, when the day became night,
When it was time to turn off the light,
Under my bed lived scary ol' Glup,
I knew he wanted to eat me up.

At 7 years old, when the day became night,
When it was time to turn off the light,
Glup appeared only when I felt sad,
With thunder and lightening, when the weather was bad.

At 8 years old, when the day became night,
When it was time to turn off the light,
Glup would just scare me now and then,
Sometimes I'd wonder where he had been.

At 9 years old, when the day became night,
When it was time to turn off the light,
I found I seldom thought of ol' Glup.
That year, it seemed, he rarely showed up.

At 10 years old, when the day became night,
When it was time to turn off the light,
I slept so soundly without a care,
And hardly remembered when Glup had been there.

At 30 years old, when the day became night,
When it was time to turn off the light,
My child cried, "Monster" and I just had to grin,
I knew my friend, Glup, was back again.

Brace Yourself!

Everyone's staring at our two faces,
Because between them there are no spaces.
I'm hoping you WON'T,
I'm warning you DON'T,
Kiss somebody when you're both wearing braces!

The Cats' Picnic

The cats awoke from their spot in the sun,
And thought that a picnic sounded like fun.
All of their friends, they would need to invite,
To leave someone out, would not be polite.
The first on the list was the small hairy dog,
Then they invited the sheep and the hog.
Next was the mule, then the sleek, black horse,
They couldn't forget Mrs. Cow, of course.
Also the goat and the big, white goose,
And how about Mr. and Mrs. Moose?
Rodney the rooster and Helen the hen,
And the fox in his den, down in the glen.
The ducks, the rabbits and the elegant swan…
But wait! Some friends did not get along.
This might be something to worry about,
So they sat and tried to figure it out.
The cats knew that <u>they'd</u> be chased by the dog,
And the sheep didn't like the big, fat hog.
The mule enjoyed kicking the horse when they'd plow,
And the goat enjoyed butting poor Mrs. Cow.
Mr. and Mrs. Moose ate too much,
They were rarely invited to parties and such.
And thinking about the rest of the bunch,
The fox would like to eat them for lunch.
So the picnic was canceled, it wouldn't be fun,
And the cats spent the day asleep in the sun.

The Caves at Camp Delight

If you hike at Camp Delight,
The caves, I've heard, are a wondrous sight.
And as you explore,
You can certainly ignore,
Those stories that **one** has an appetite.

Carwash

The town's new carwash is quite unique,
It seems they're using a new technique.
The amount of water the carwash has drunk,
Determines the force of spray from his trunk.

My car has never been so clean,
It's the best carwash I've ever seen.
You'll never have to pay a dime,
He works for peanuts every time!

Bubblehead

I knew a boy named Steven Strum,
Who always swallowed his bubble gum.
I heard there were bubbles all over the place,
Emerging from every hole in his face.
Bubbles were coming out of his nose,
And from his mouth, so his mouth couldn't close.
Bubbles and bubbles from both of his ears,
His eyes had bubbles that looked like big tears.
His head puffed up, and it's hard to figure,
That Steven's head could get any bigger.
But, what I heard, and it's duly noted,
At some point in time, his head exploded.

This can't be true about Steven Strum,
But will I swallow my bubble gum?
Certainly not! I'm not that dumb!

Carrot Top

I thought they called him Carrot Top,
Because his hair was red.
But I soon found out,
What that name was about,
When he removed his hat from his head.

Brains

I blew and blew and blew my nose,
Then blew and blew some more.
I guess I blew a little too hard,
'Cause my brains fell on the floor.

I'm not even sure I can finish this poem,
I *think* I'm going insane.
But that is just impossible,
I can't *think* without a brain!

Escargot

Escargot or snail,
Call them by either name.
To eat one is disgusting,
I think they feel the same.

Lucky Penny

Hip, Hip, Hip Hooray!
I found a lucky penny today!
It was on the ground next to a tree,
I bent to get it and skinned my knee.
As I stood up with my knee so red,
A branch was low and I bumped my head.
As I fell backwards, I split my pants,
And then I found I was covered in ants.
I'm lucky they weren't the biting kind,
So you see, that penny was a lucky find.

How Many Licks are in My Sucker?

I got to one-hundred, someone knocked on the door,
Beginning again, I licked two-hundred and four.

I got confused at two-hundred and ten.
Did that first one-hundred get counted in?

So I added one-hundred to two-hundred and ten,
The licking and counting began again.

It didn't take long to lose my place.
Was all this counting a hopeless case?

It looked like I was halfway through,
I'd start at zero and multiply by two!

So this time I counted to four-hundred and four,
Quite a bit higher than I counted before.

The sucker was gone, the licking was done.
It really hadn't been all that much fun.

So, how many licks? Seven-hundred and three?
I have a headache. Please don't ask me!

Brain Overload

My brain is full, it's on overload.
I can't put another thing in, it's true.
So I tip my head and give it a bump,
To spill out the old and make room for what's new.

My Tooth Ith Looth

My tooth ith looth.
What can I thay?
It'th been like thith
For theven dayth.

It muth come out.
It muth be thoon.
I thurp a thtraw,
Can't uthe a thpoon.

I cannot thand
Thith anymore
I'll tie a thring,
And thlam the door.

My tooth came out!!
I can talk, juth lithen…

I gueth I muth wait
Till my tooth grothe back in!

Brussel Sprouts

"I like Brussel Sprouts for dinner," said Sue.
"I like them in my salad," said Clyde.
When asked where **I** like Brussel Sprouts,
"Down the garbage disposal," I replied.

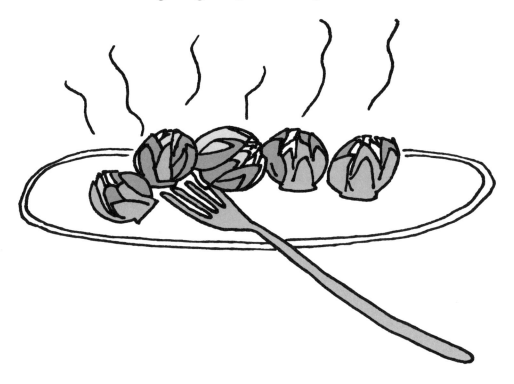

Small Fry

The French Fry race had finally begun.
Everyone was having fun!
The curly fries had started fast,
They didn't want to come in last.
The chili fries came 'round the bend,
Running quickly to the race's end.
The cheesy fries had slowed to a stop,
They struck a pose for a photo-op!
Late in the race, what did we find?
The little fry was way behind.
Through the noise of the cheering crowd,
The little fry proclaimed out loud,
As the final stretch was coming up,
"I DON'T NEED TO WIN... JUST 'KETCHUP'!"

Julie Jessica's Bad Hair Year

Julie Jessica just didn't care.
She never ever washed her hair.

It became a home for flies and bees,
Wiggly spiders, bugs and fleas.

As her hair grew long, it became congested,
With worms and ants, it became infested.

A bird made a nest way up on the top,
Yet, Julie still wouldn't wash that mop.

It became quite crowded as the year went by,
When everything started to multiply.

Then one day, Julie noticed them thinning.
She saw a web the spiders were spinning.

They had trapped the flies and bugs and bees,
And the bird had eaten the ants, worms, and fleas.

The bird finished up with a last spider snack,
And flew on up to her nest to pack.

Gone was the food and so was she.
The bird flew away to live in a tree.

Now that the critters had left her hair,
Do you think that Julie decided to care?

Nope... She still never ever washed her hair.

Tent

I pop it open,
Climb inside.
I feel so safe,
My place to hide.

I have what I need
To spend the night.
My sleeping bag,
A bright flashlight.

It's quiet outside,
I don't hear a peep.
I snuggle on in,
And try to sleep.

I hear a noise,
Outside my tent.
Maybe a bear,
Picked up my scent!

Now the footsteps
Are coming near!
If I keep quiet,
It won't find me here.

I suddenly feel
A sense of doom...
My sister then yells,
"Get out of my room!!"

Dirty Clothes Band

The dirty blue jeans stood in the corner,
Wishing that they were clean.
Smelly and stiff, they stood all alone,
And longed for the washing machine.

To make them complete, the dirty blue jeans
Were joined by a shirt, socks and shoes.
Together they formed The Dirty Clothes Band,
And sang 'The Dirty Clothes Blues'.

One day the outfit crept through the house.
It must have been such a strange sight.
But they made a mistake in the laundry room,
Not separating dark clothes from light.

They've changed their name to The Clean Clothes Band,
The blue jeans, shirt, socks and shoes.
But now they sing a different tune,
The 'Same Shade of Blue Clothes Blues'.

Kite

My brother asked if I'd help fly a kite,
I replied, "I don't see why?
Why do you stand with a string in your hand,
Just staring up in the sky?"

"It's such a boring waste of time,
There are better things to do.
I'm sure I can find ten reasons why,
I won't fly a kite with you."

But it seems I helped him anyway,
Although I protested so.
He attached a tail and up I did sail.
I hope he doesn't let go.

Moooooon

Do you remember that cute little tune,
About how the cow jumped over the moon?

A cow?! The moon?! How can that be?
We all know a cow can't jump over a **tree**!

Unless, perhaps, her speed was transonic,
Or maybe even supersonic.

And we must consider some other things,
Like the lift drag ratio of the cow's wings.

A cow with wings? That's silly, of course.
But needed to conquer aerodynamic force.

There's fuel consumption, ionization,
And also molecular dissociation.

And stagnation pressure or velocity,
Don't forget the surface catalycity.

And then there are things that can get in the way,
Like "space junk" due to orbital decay.

But stranger things have happened in space,
Like why does the moon seem to have a face?

So whenever we hear a sonic boom,
Let's imagine a cow has reached the moon.

UFO? Moo-F-O?

Oh my gosh! Did you see that cow?
It flew across the sky just now.
You didn't see that cow fly by?
I thought I saw it in the sky.
I guess the sky **is** a bit hazy.
"I'd better be quiet, they'll think I'm crazy."

Silence is Golden

A snake met a friend by the garden wall,
But the snake's new friend didn't talk at all.
But that was all right,
'Cause they'd never fight.
Their friendship lasted from Spring till Fall.

Maggie McClain

Let me explain how Maggie McClain,
One day slipped down the shower drain.

She refused to eat dinner, not one bite went in her,
And each day Maggie got thinner and thinner!

As the story goes, first went her toes,
Then knees and hands and arms and nose.

And since that day, I've heard people say.
Poor Maggie McClain must have lost her way.

Everyone knew, she had slipped clear through,
And floated away on the ocean blue.

My story's complete, the end not so sweet.
All because Maggie McClain wouldn't eat!

Elephant Stew

Why is there an elephant
In my bowl of stew?
Did one recently escape
From the city zoo?

How am I supposed to eat?
He takes up all the space.
Stew is sloshing all about,
And messing up the place!

My spoon won't fit beside him,
I'm very hungry, too.
How am I supposed to eat,
With an elephant in my stew?!!

Bigfoot

Bigfoot had a party,
He didn't invite me at all.
He said I wasn't hairy enough,
And my feet were way too small.
He said his friends smell really bad,
And stand about ten feet tall.
He said my voice is just too soft,
His friends have a blood curdling call.
And the parties can be quite wild,
He says they have a ball.
Although they haven't hurt anyone yet,
Some folks, they might want to maul!

I hope if he has more parties,
He doesn't invite me at all.

Quicksand

I'm
  being
    swallowed
      by
        quicksand!
         All
          that
           are
            left
             are
              my
               head
                and
                 a
                  (blub)
                   (blub)...

Fruit Salad

At nine, I ate a ripe banana.
At ten, I ate a bunch.
At eleven, I ate a watermelon.
At twelve, six apples for lunch.

At one, I ate a very sweet orange.
At two, a bunch of cherries.
At three, I ate a cantaloupe.
At four, I ate some berries.

At five, Mom made a big fruit salad.
I felt a little crummy.
I had to tell her, "None for me,
I made one in my tummy."

Spot

I hugged my dog, my face got hot,
And on my chin, appeared a spot.
Mom called the doctor, "Bring her on in,
I'd like to see that spot on her chin."

We got in the car, I closed the door.
I started to itch and got three more.
Driving through town, past houses and trees,
As I looked down, I saw spots on my knees.

While putting the car in the parking space,
Ten more spots showed up on my face!
"Okay, we're here," my mom then said.
I felt eight spots pop out on my head.

Out of the car and onto the street,
I saw I now had spots on my feet.
I heard the doc say, as I walked in,
"Let's have a look at that spot on her chin."

"Whoa!" he said, as he took a look.
And then he ran to look in his book.
"I think I've found just what you've got.
It won't hurt much, but you need a shot."

Where that very first spot appeared on my chin,
Now, no spot was there on my skin.
I looked at the place of that very first spot,
The spot was gone, not even a dot!

One by one, the spots disappeared,
Dot by dot, my complexion cleared.
"What was it doc? What have I got?"
"You're allergic to dogs."

"You mean my dog, Spot?!"

Ouch!

Sally McGee skinned her knee.
Cousin Ken bruised his shin.
Billy Stump bumped his rump.
Sister Lynn hurt her chin.
Katie Karm scraped her arm.
Billy Boze stubbed his toes.
Brother Fred fell on his head.
Auntie Rose smashed her nose.
But my friend Burt, skid in the dirt,
Stumbled, tumbled, fell and fumbled.
And somehow Burt never got hurt.

My Invisible Friend

I have an invisible friend,
Who helps me everyday.

Sometimes he does my homework,
When I go out to play.

So if my homework is right,
The credit for that I'll claim.

But if my homework is wrong,
My invisible friend is to blame.

Potatoes

"You'd better wash," Mom warned me for years,
"Or potatoes will grow inside of your ears!"
I know my mom is really wise,
But I didn't expect to grow French Fries!!

Super Hero?

I've got the cape,
And a super tan.
I've got the tights,
I'm Superman!

I've got an "S"
On my super chest.
I know I'm better,
Than the super rest!

I climb so high,
With ease, yes I can!
Now watch me fly...
I'm Superman!!

But I fall straight down,
What a stupid plan!
Oh yeah, I forgot,
I'm Super **Stan**.

Cheese

The little furry mouse, Louise,
Chewed in and out through a block of cheese.
But no one found anything amiss,
Instead of Cheddar, they assumed it was Swiss.

Cruisin'

Bobby's skates are red,
Dan's skateboard is blue.
Erin's trike has three wheels,
Lindsay's bike has two.
Ryan rides a scooter,
Kayla rides a mule.
Jocelyn rides on roller blades,
All the way to school.
Chandra rides a surfboard,
And hopes she won't wipeout.
Taylor has a golf cart,
She drives it all about.
Melissa rides a horse,
Whose coat is shiny black.
Chad drives a pick-up truck,
With a camper on the back.
Crista rides a motorbike,
On which she likes to cruise.
Me, I'm not so lucky,
I travel on my shoes.

I'm Snazzy!

It's the first day of school and I'm happy to say,
I've waited and waited for this special day!

Wait till the kids get a good look at me!
I'm looking as snazzy as I can be!

My backpack, notebook, and pens are new.
My shirt, my hat, and jacket are too.

My hair is cut in the lastest style.
My face is wearing a winning smile.

New socks and shoes, all clean and bright,
I know that I am quite a sight!

I'm wondering if I should have made a list.
I somehow feel that something was missed.

I guess I'm as ready as I'll ever be.
The looks on their faces, I can't wait to see.

I'm running late, but I really don't mind,
I'll walk into class just a little behind.

Soup

"What's for dinner?" I asked my mom.
"Soup," is what she said.
Visions of Mom's homemade creations,
Deliciously danced through my head.

Her pumpkin squash is out of this world,
And how can I describe her potato?
Her nine-bean soup is widely known,
And so is her tomato.

But today I had an enormous craving,
Clam chowder I was hopin'.
I asked, "Which soup?" and she replied,
"Whichever one you open."

Mixed-Up Family

I have Grandma's eyes, or so I've been told,
I've heard that since I was two years old.
And Auntie's long fingers, and Uncle's long toes,
Daddy's long legs, and Sister's short nose.
Grandpa's sweet smile, and Brother's strong chin,
And they're sure I have Great-Grandmother's skin.
My voice is Mommy's when sweetly she sings,
Wait!! What will *they* do without all of these things???

Finger Food

Sneaky Lynn Diana Cole,
Liked sticking her finger in the sugar bowl.
But that was not the very worst,
She always licked that finger first.

Parade

I really enjoyed the parade today,
I sat on the curb and waved a flag.
My balloon got loose, disappeared in the sky,
Just as a funny clown came by.
There was something about that clown's disguise,
That frightened me some, so I closed my eyes.
The marching bands brought me to tears,
They were so loud, I covered my ears.
A unicycle ran over my shoe,
I looked at my foot, it was black and blue.
I ate cotton candy till my stomach hurt,
My ice-cream cone fell into the dirt.
My hat blew off exposing my head,
The sun beat down till my head got red.
I wish we could have a parade everyday,
'Cause I really enjoyed the parade today.

The Juggler

I can juggle three balls and spin a ring on my toe!
It's easy, there's nothing to it.
One, two, three! Watch, here I go!
Oops! I didn't say how long I could do it.

Smart Swine

I have the most amazing pig,
He knows so many things.
He stands up and does a jig,
And opens his mouth and sings.

My awesome pig can also play
Checkers, poker and chess.
And at these games, I have to say,
In the barnyard, he's the best.

I know my pig is very smart,
And considers me his best friend.
I know he holds me dear in his heart,
'Cause sometimes he lets me win!

Meow

I work so hard watching the yard
For gophers digging their holes.
I sit for hours through sunshine and showers,
Waiting and watching for moles.

They're such little pests and make a big mess,
"Come out of that hole," I dare.
Twitching an ear as a fly buzzes near,
For hours, I continue to stare.

Not feeling nice, I "meow" once or twice
To fill that gopher with fear.
Then let him forget, as I patiently sit,
And wait for him to appear.

Day after day, from June through May,
The yard is where I'm at.
Through lightening and thunder, I often wonder,
Why don't I just get a cat??!

I'm So Sorry

I'm so sorry for what I've done,
I'd like to take it back.
What has happened is all my fault,
The sky has just turned black.

I couldn't sleep at all last night,
And morning came too soon.
I threw a rock at that bright yellow sun,
And it hid behind the moon!

Dog-Gone-It!

How does a dog cope with life's highs and lows,
When there are only seconds between?
His happiest moment is when the bowl's full,
And saddest when he's licked that bowl clean!

Just One Sandwich

The "one sandwich diet" was what the doctor
Prescribed for Mr. Dyke.
"What kind?" he asked. And the doctor replied,
"Whatever kind you like."

On that diet, he ate just one sandwich
Everyday for quite some time.
But every time he stepped on the scale,
He'd watch the numbers climb.

Also, he noticed that all of his clothes
Seemed to be getting so tight.
He figured they must have shrunk in the dryer.
Of course, that had to be right.

"Okay," he thought, "My scale is broken,
And my dryer is on the blink.
I know I can explain everything else,
But how did my front door shrink?"

Dinner

Last night, I went to dinner
At the house of my new friend.
The night was so unusual,
The details I'll extend...

There were a couple of turkey legs,
A head of lettuce and two pigs feet.
An artichoke heart and ears of corn,
And lady-fingers that looked so sweet.

A round pork shoulder, a large cow's tongue,
A lobster tail, but let me add,
Enough about describing my friend,
Now I'll describe the dinner we had....

I Own a Cat

She sleeps on my bed,
The middle is her place.
I cling to the edge,
To give her more space.

She purrs in my ear,
Till I get out of bed.
She meows at me,
Until she is fed.

When she wants to go out,
I open the door.
When she wants the chair,
I sit on the floor.

Her favorite sport,
Is chasing a mouse.
Or chasing the dog,
Around the house.

She sharpens her claws,
On anything there,
The sofa, the rug,
My favorite chair.

She sleeps all day,
Then stops for a bite,
Then curls right up,
And sleeps all night.

With attitude,
That of course, she flaunts,
She always does,
Whatever she wants.

I love her dearly,
That's plain to see.
I own a cat,
Or does **she** own me?

Mean Kid

Who put a grasshopper down Emmy Lou's back?
A mean kid, that's who.
Who painted the dining room table black?
A mean kid, that's who.
Who put gum in Elizabeth's hair?
A mean kid, that's who.
Who put tacks on the Principal's chair?
A mean kid, that's who.
Who put the goldfish in the toilet bowl?
A mean kid, that's who.
Who put glue in the donut hole?
A mean kid, that's who.
Who put a frog in the teacher's desk drawer?
A mean kid, that's who.
Who glued the cat to the living room floor?
A mean kid, that's who.
Who opened presents on December 21st?
A mean kid, that's who.
In a "Nice Kid Contest", who was voted the worst?
Mean kid, Me! That's who!

Celery

Have you heard about the celery stalk,
That grew a mouth and learned to talk?
It learned to sing a splendid ballad,
But still ended up in someone's salad.

Cough-A-Doodle-Doo!

Cough-a-doodle,
Cough-a-doodle,
The rooster has the flu.
And to top it off,
Because of the cough,
He let me sleep till two!

Cough-a-doodle,
Cough-a-doodle,
He's too sick to leave the coop.
To make him feel better,
I took him a sweater,
And a bowl of chicken soup.

Home Sweet Home

The little ant's home was very dark,
Situated squarely in the middle of a park.

With plenty of food, he never complained.
His home stayed dry whenever it rained.

Sometimes the sun came shining in,
Then quick as a flash, it was dark again.

For a party, his friends came over one day,
They liked it there and decided to stay.

They called their uncles, cousins and aunts,
Hundreds and hundreds of little black ants.

What would he feed them? What would they eat?
His question was answered, in a heartbeat.

His roof opened up and food tumbled in,
Half-eaten hot dogs and fried chicken skin.

Watermelon rinds all covered with cake,
Beans mixed with soda and barbecued steak.

Word got around about this retreat.
More ants came to party and also to eat.

How did they find him, his party, this bash?
They were all told to go to the home labeled "**TRASH**".

My Teacher's from Mars

My teacher's from Mars,
Please don't be misled,
I know she has eyes
In the back of her head.

With her back to the class,
"I'm watching," she'll say.
How can this be?
There's no other way.

No one has seen them,
But **I** know they're there.
Hidden quite well
Beneath her long hair.

Now you've been warned,
You're always in view...
I'm beginning to think,
My mom's from Mars, too!

Huge Purple Thing

What is this thing on the side of my face?
This huge purple thing that is taking up space.
It's been here so long,
It doesn't belong,
It's absolutely, positively in the wrong place.

What is this thing? Is it here to stay?
It arrived, let's see, I've forgotten which day.
Night after night,
It's such a bad sight.
Wait! Never mind. It just crawled away!

Sleeping Bag

The sleeping bag lay on the floor,
Not making a single peep.
I tiptoed past that sleeping bag,
Because it was asleep.

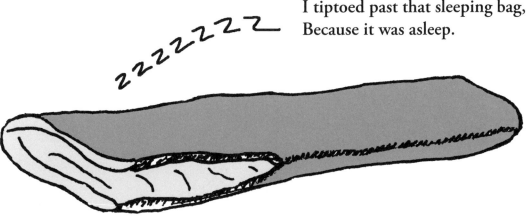

Chicken?!

I heard we were having chicken for dinner.
I like it fried the best.
But it wasn't fried, or even baked,
That chicken was our guest!

Rock-Solid Friendship

Said the rock by the road,
"What will my life hold?
I'd love to roll from this space.
Or will this spot be my life's abode,
And I'll never go anyplace?"

Said the rock by the road,
"I feel so alone,
Without a family or friend.
Not a single pebble or even a stone,
When will this loneliness end?"

Said the rock by the road,
"It's getting quite cold,
A storm is starting to brew."
Lightening struck! He's no longer alone,
'Cause it split that rock in two.

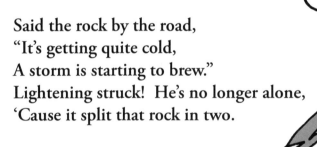

Stuck

I'm sitting here staring at the wall and the paint.
I know I'm here, but I know what ain't.
If I had one wish, just what would it be?
At this very moment, that's easy for me.
A toilet paper roll that would never run out,
I could then get up and walk all about.
So I'm sitting here feeling a bit out of luck,
Now you know where I am, and you know why I'm stuck!!

Depressed

My eyes are stuck shut,
My ears are flapped down,
My nose is closed tight,
My mouth has a frown.

My hands are both flat,
My feet turn away,
If **you** see a steamroller,
GET OUT OF THE WAY!!

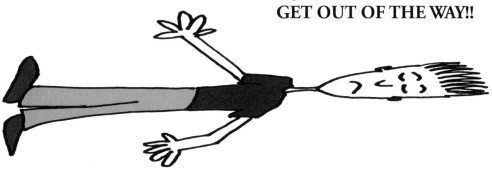

A Dog's Life

I dig up the garden everyday,
Their shoes I love to chew.
I jump on them with muddy paws,
It's okay, they expect me to.

I bark at night when they're trying to sleep,
I tear up a cushion or two.
Sometimes I forget and pee on the floor,
It's okay, they expect me to.

One day I ate the banana cream pie,
One day I ate the stew,
One day I ate the Sloppy Joes,
It's okay, they expect me to.

Sometimes I hear, "What did you do?!"
But it's followed by a hug or two.
I know they love me in spite of it all,
They're my family, I expect them to.

Skiing

I thought that I'd go skiing,
And headed for the slope.
But I was too late, or a bit too soon,
It was 90 degrees and the middle of June!
I feel like such a dope.

Ostrich

This isn't too hard to understand,
I look like an ostrich with it's head in the sand.
Part is true of what you just read,
I am an ostrich, but I have no head.

Blade O'Grass

Blade woke up feeling fresh and strong,
He hoped his family wouldn't sleep too long.
The sun was shining, they'd be up soon,
He knew they had haircuts scheduled for noon.
They all had a shower just yesterday,
And a luncheon was planned after haircuts today.

Soon the O'Grasses were all standing straight,
Blade was happy they had not been late.
They heard a motor as it raced, then slowed,
It was time, they knew, for them all to be mowed.
Then, with all their new haircuts complete,
A fertilizer luncheon would then be their treat!

Skates

My brand new skates are the fastest in town.
My brand new skates are the fastest around.
But whoever made them made some mistakes,
My brand new skates don't have any braaaaaaaakes........!

Human Pretzel

One day in gym class, my teacher said,
"I want each of you to stand on your head."

"We'll start with you," and she pointed at me.
Stand on my head?! How could that be?!

Stand on my head?! Did <u>she</u> have a clue?
Was that even something my body could do?

Nervously, I began to sweat,
My hands and feet began to get wet.

Everyone waited for me to perform,
My stomach hurt, and my head got warm.

I could stand on the floor, I could stand on the bed,
But how could I possibly stand on my head?

How would this work? I just didn't know,
When my head was up here and my feet down below.

I laid on the mat and twisted around,
None of the kids made a single sound.

They watched, amazed, that I could thread
My feet through my arms, till they touched my head.

I tried to stand up so straight and tall,
With my feet on my head, but I started to fall.

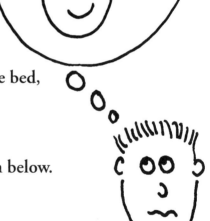

I tried once again and got all tangled,
My arms and legs were strangely angled.

My teacher's mouth was frozen in place,
With a look of awe upon her face.

They tried to untangle me all that day,
But that didn't happen, and I stayed that way.

It turned out okay, for now I've found fame,
'The Human Pretzel' is **now** my new name.

Broken Arm

I broke my arm,
The cast is fine.
An excellent place,
For friends to sign.
There's no more room,
What can I do?
Perhaps I should break,
The other one, too.

Splat!

Oh seagull, how you like to pretend,
That you want to be my very best friend.
But you're not truthful, I have a hunch,
All you really want is my lunch.
I'm happy to share, so here is a bite,
He grabs that piece and then takes flight.
All at once, I'm surrounded by others,
His friends, his cousins and their mothers!
Their flocking all above my head,
They must have heard about the one I fed.
How the good news has traveled fast,
It seems that only a minute has passed.
Twenty, forty, sixty or more,
Too many now for me to ignore.
How I wish these birds would retreat,
And leave me alone so that I can eat.
It's usually fun to eat outdoors... SPLAT!
Here you go birds, my sandwich is now yours!!

Wet World

The world got all wet today.
That's why I couldn't go out to play.
I sat all alone inside my room,
Feeling so sad and filled with gloom,
Because the world got all wet today.

The world got all wet today.
The sky became so dark and gray.
But the rivers and the streams are flowing,
The world outside is green and growing,
Because the world got all wet today.

The world got all wet today.
Plants and trees got a drink from the spray.
The crops will grow into food we'll eat,
Flowers can bloom and smell so sweet,
Because the world got all wet today.

The world got all wet today.
So, if I get thirsty anytime of the day,
I can turn on the faucet in the sink,
And simply get myself a drink,
Because the world got all wet today.

The world got all wet today.
After thinking about it, I'm feeling okay.
The beautiful world is so alive,
Our wonderful world can now survive,
Because the world got all wet today.

Speak!

Your dog must be smarter than mine,
He dances on two feet.
He shakes, rolls over, and begs,
Whenever you give him a treat.

My dog only knows one trick,
When I give her treats and such.
And then, when I ask my dog to speak,
She says, "Thank you very much."

A, B, Z's

Memorizing the alphabet,
Wasn't easy for Lee.
Whenever he'd get halfway through,
He'd go directly to Zzzzzzzz.

What's in a Name?

My parents gave me a beautiful name,
"Anita" is lovely, I shouldn't complain.
I was told not to be a fusser or fumer,
My parents, I know, had a great sense of humor.
It's not the first name that has caused me such pain,
It's the first, along with my strange last name.
How could a name be such a big deal?
As 'Anita Kiss', how would you feel?

Surf's Up

My surfboard's ready,
My wetsuit too.
A surfing trip
Is way overdue.

I cannot wait
To walk the nose,
Hang 5 and 10
With all my toes.

I'll shoot the curl,
And shoot the tube.
I know I'm cool,
I'm a surfer dude!

The waves are gnarly,
I'm totally stoked.
If I wipe out,
I'll be totally soaked.

On my board,
I can really cook.
I learned to surf
From a "how to" book.

I have my towel,
And suntan lotion.
Just one thing's missing,
And that's an ocean!!

Trick or Treat

Poor Randy Blake made a big mistake,
One foggy Halloween night.
The costume he chose,
Was a great big nose.
What a ridiculous sight!

He walked all around the streets of the town,
But his costume became an issue.
'Cause what they gave Randy,
Was certainly not candy,
Just cotton swabs and tissue.

Hats

Many hats were standing in line.
To the first, the second hat said,
"Do you mind if I cut in front of you?
I'm in a hurry and must get a head."

We're Off Like a Dirty Shirt

"We're off like a dirty shirt," Dad would say,
Each time we'd take a trip away.
But first a long, long list we'd make,
Of things to do and things to take.
Wash the car and fill up the tank,
Pick up some money from the bank.
Water the plants and mow the lawn,
Hurry, so we can leave by dawn.
Pack the car for our get-away fling,
Let's not forget a single thing.
Save some room for the dog in the car,
The parakeet, and Dad's guitar.
Pack your socks and your underwear,
Choose your clothes with lots of care.
Pajamas, slippers and toothbrush,
Time's getting short, we need to rush.
Camera, binoculars, and hiking boots,
Swim fins, snorkel gear, and bathing suits.
And other things for fun in the sun,
Beachball, inner tubes…I only found one.
Remember the kite and lots of string,
Hats and sunglasses, don't miss a thing.
Be sure to pack the food we'll need,
And food for the dog, and the parakeet seed.
Ice chest with ice and juice to drink,
Seems like everything but the kitchen sink.
Camp stove, lantern, and bug spray,
Flashlight and batteries, now don't delay.
Our sleeping bags and tent, we'll need,
Writing pads, pens, and books to read.
Pots and pans, forks, spoons and knives,
And ointment in case we break out in hives.

A campfire at night is what we love most,
Bring matches, wood, and marshmallows to toast.
And what if it should happen to pour?
Pack the umbrellas, I think we need four.
Ask the neighbor to pick up the mail,
Also the newspaper. Now let's hit the trail!
"We're off like a dirty shirt," Dad would say,
Each time we'd take off for our trip of one day.

From Here To There

How do you get from here to there?
I have a few concerns.
Like how far **there** is away from **here**,
And how many twists and turns.

And what if I happen to lose my way,
When traveling from here to there?
Before starting out I'd like to know,
Where **here** is and where is **there**?

I thought it would help to ask directions,
To be sure and ease my fear.
But the man I asked, scratched his head and said,
"You know, you can't get there from here."

Shrimp

Why do you call me a shrimp?
I know I'm not so tall.
Why do you call me a shrimp?
I know I am quite small.
Why do you call me shrimp?
I'm only just a kid.
Why do you call me a shrimp?
'Cause I happen to be a squid.

Crab Fest

Whoop and Holler! Scream and Screech!
Our annual Crab Fest is underway!
As we all run down to the beach,
The crabs all run the other way!

Fog Monster

The Fog Monster rolls all through the town,
On dark and moonless nights.
Covering buildings, roads and cars,
Whatever is in it's sight.

I heard it doesn't care what it eats,
Nothing is safe in it's path.
Better watch out, I'm warning you,
Beware of the Fog Monster's wrath.

It's massive arms can surround a town,
And make it disappear.
You'll never see that town again,
At least, that's what I hear.

Oh no! It's creeping down my block!
I see it's devouring a tree.
And now it's eating up my house,
And NOW IT'S EATING MEEEEEEEEEE.........

Who Wrote This Crazy Book?

Who wrote this crazy book?
The words are upside down.
The cover and the pictures, too,
The faces wear a frown.

Whoever wrote this crazy book,
Must be so very smart.
And to draw the pictures upside down,
Is quite a work of art.

Hat's off to the author,
And illustrator as well.
How will I ever read this book?
It's really hard to tell...

At last, I have it figured out!
This book has now been read.
The writer's smart, but I'm much smarter,
I simply stood on my head.

Index

A, B, Z's	115
A Dog's Life	103
Arf Mail	20-21
Bigfoot	66-67
Blade O'Grass	106
Bottomless Pit Pete	7
Brace Yourself	32-33
Brain Overload	47
Brains	43
Bricks	19
Broken Arm	110
Brussel Sprouts	50
Bubblehead	40-41
Carrot Top	42
Carwash	38-39
The Cats' Picnic	34-35
The Caves At Camp Delight	36-37
Celery	94
Cheese	76
Chicken?!	100
Cough-A-Doodle-Doo!	95
Crab Fest	124
Cruisin'	77
Depressed	102
Dinner	90
Dirty Clothes Band	56-57
Dog-Gone-It!	87

Elephant Stew	64-65
Escargot	44
Finger Food	81
Flying Pieces of Macaroni & Cheese	2-3
Fog Monster	125
From Here To There	122
Fruit Salad	69
Fudge	17
Glup	30-31
The "Gotcha"	14-15
Hats	119
Help!	10-11
Helping Hand	13
Home Sweet Home	96-97
Hot Dog!	8
How Many Licks are in My Sucker?	46
Huge Purple Thing	99
Human Pretzel	108-109
I Own a Cat	91
Identity Crisis	9
I'm Snazzy!	78-79
I'm So Sorry	86
The Juggler	83
Julie Jessica's Bad Hair Year	52-53
Just One Sandwich	88-89

Kite	58-59	Shrimp	123
		Silence Is Golden	62
Lonely Spider	4	Skates	107
Lucky Penny	45	Skiing	104
		Sleeping Bag	99
Maggie McClain	63	Small Fry	51
Mean Kid	92-93	Smart Swine	84
Meow	85	Soup	80
Merry McQuid	6	Speak!	114
Mixed-Up Family	81	Splat!	111
Moooooon	60-61	Spot	70-71
Motorcycle Minnie	12	Stuck	102
My Invisible Friend	73	Summer Vacation	26-27
My Stuff	24-25	Super Hero?	75
My Teacher's from Mars	98	Surf's Up	116-117
My Tooth Ith Looth	48-49		
		Tent	54-55
Nuts	16	Trick or Treat	118
		The Twister Of Fear	5
Ostrich	105		
Ouch!	72	UFO? Moo-F-O?	61
Parade	82	Violent Chef	28
Potatoes	74		
		We're Off Like A Dirty Shirt	120-121
Quicksand	68	Wet World	112-113
		What's In A Name?	115
Remember To Forget	18	Who Wrote This Crazy Book?	126-127
Ring-a-Ding	22-23		
Rock-Solid Friendship	101		
Rollercoaster?	29		

From Jeanne...

In loving memory of my dad, Ernest (Smitty) Smither, whose wit and humor shows up everywhere in this book. Thanks, Dad.

Also, thank you to my family and friends for supplying me with years of funny memories which have woven their way in and out through every page. And, for your constant encouragement throughout the past year to keep me on track in completing this book. It's a dream come true!

Thank you to my mom, Rayma, my husband, Efrem, and my dear friend, Merry, for your hours of intense proofreading, and for laughing in all the right places. Also, thank you to Lisa, for jumping on board from the beginning and becoming my illustrator and business partner, and for your endearing illustrations which have made the poems come alive.

Lastly, love to my grandchildren, Kyle and Katherine... May you cherish this book forever.

From Lisa...

First of all, thank you to my husband, Mark, and my children, Kyle and Katherine, for your love and support.

AND, to my dad, "Papa Efrem", for your incredible patience, love, and unselfish time and devotion to Kyle and Katherine! We couldn't do it all without you!

A great big THANK YOU to Sarah Davis for all of your technical advice and assistance. You are a wealth of knowledge!

But, MOST OF ALL, the biggest thanks goes back to my mom for being so creative and witty!